CHARACTER ALL LEADERS MUST HAVE

Becoming a
Person of Integrity

LIFE IMPACT SERIES

FRANK DAMAZIO

CityChristianPublishing

www.CityChristianPublishing.com

PUBLISHED BY CITY CHRISTIAN PUBLISHING
9200 NE Fremont, Portland, Oregon 97220

City Christian Publishing is a ministry of City Bible Church and is dedicated to serving the local church and its leaders through the production and distribution of quality equipping resources. It is our prayer that these materials, proven in the context of the local church, will equip leaders in exalting the Lord and extending His kingdom.

For a free catalog of additional resources from City Christian Publishing, please call 1-800-777-6057 or visit our web site at www.citychristianpublishing.com.

Character All Leaders Must Have
© Copyright 2005 by Frank Damazio
All Rights Reserved
ISBN: 1-59383-028-9

Cover design by DesignPoint, Inc.
Interior design and typeset by Katherine Lloyd, Bend, Oregon.

All Scripture quotations, unless otherwise indicated, are taken from The King James Version of the Bible. In some Scripture references, italics have added by the author for emphasis.
Other versions used are:
AMP–*Amplified Bible.* © 1965, 1987, by Zondervan Publishing House.
NIV–*Holy Bible, New International* Version. © 1973, 1978, 1984
by International Bible Society.
NKJV–*New King James Version.* © 1979, 1980, 1982
by Thomas Nelson, Inc. Publishers.

First Edition, July 2005
Printed in the United States of America

Table of Contents

Chapter One

FULFILLING OR FORFEITING YOUR CALLING

$\mathcal{H}$orace Mann once said: "Character is what God and the angels know of us; reputation is what men and women think of us." Have you ever thought about what God sees when he looks into the very depth of your being? What kind of person does he find in you? Are you loving, generous, and hardworking, or are you full of bitterness, anger, and self-gratification? Who you are determines how you will respond to any and every situation, whether good or bad, positive or negative.

God's purposes for, or determination of, your destiny, is a result of His foreknowledge. Yet, His divine will and plan for your life is conditional. It is based upon your cooperation. Every person has genuine options, and as each choice is made, God responds accordingly. The freedom to fulfill God's design over your life is determined by your ability to choose options in light of your character.

The destiny of all people lies in a finite balance of God's sovereignty and human responsibility. God is in control of all circumstances that may bear upon a person's life, but ultimately each one is responsible for responding correctly, godly, and biblically. Your response in various situations will inevitably determine the character that you will possess. Whether it is acting in love, forgiveness, bitterness, cold-heartedness, happiness, joy, sorrow, or anger, a fundamental principle in God's economy is that your actions will affect the lives of all those whom you may one day lead in a dramatic way. To fully understand what we are talking about here, let us draw from the life example of Reuben.

Reuben was a leader who forfeited his high calling in God by making choices that negated God's plan for his life. He refused to correct a blatant character flaw that was later passed down to his successors, resulting in a tragic waste of awesome leadership potential. This is captured in Genesis 49:3-4, when Jacob, the father of the twelve tribes of Israel, called forth his sons and prophesied over them. Beginning with Reuben, he said: "You are my firstborn, my might, the first sign of my strength, excelling in honor, excelling in power. Turbulent as the waters, you will no longer excel, for you went up onto your father's bed, onto my couch and defiled it (NIV)."

We see in this verse that great expectations had been formed of Reuben but he refused to answer the call. He had a double portion of the birthright and was well positioned to receive all the privileges and rights associated with this title. He stood to benefit from a great inheritance. But the awful power of sensuality became Reuben's downfall. He had an uncontrollable torrent of passion that he could not govern himself (Genesis 35:22).

From Reuben, we learn that sinful actions can remove people from positions of leadership. He destroyed his right to inherit. He displayed an instability of character. Jacob described this character flaw as "turbulent water." This term is well adapted to express the unbridled lawlessness of Reuben's conduct in the indulgence of his passions, and the effect of it in suddenly and irretrievably casting him down from his birthright. It is like the force of a great current of water that becomes irresistible when the barriers that restrained it are removed. Such is the force of corruption in men destitute of religious principle. Yet nothing is weaker than water in small

CHARACTER ALL LEADERS MUST HAVE

quantities. It has no principle of cohesion or stability. And it was this water-like instability that destroyed Reuben's ability to enjoy preeminence. He was a weak man who walked after his own lusts.

Through Reuben's life, we see that, although a person is born into greatness, there is no guarantee that he or she* will truly ever become great. It all boils down to character. Interestingly, the Hebrew word used to describe Reuben's ruinous disposition is *pahal,* meaning unstable, disregarding the godly order and acting with pride or presumption. And Reuben's character was exactly that. He was reckless and lascivious. He had a certain unbridled element, a boiling over, a seething that pervaded his every thought and motive. This was, in itself, a sure destruction.

Consequently, the moral weakness of Reuben, not just the moral sin, caused his forfeit of leadership. The single sin that made him infamous grew out of

*Unless otherwise stated, whenever the masculine gender is used, both men and women are included.

his character, confirming and establishing it in evil more and more. Thus, the thoughts, feelings, and deeds of a man—the whole of his character in the present—are made and determined by his past. Sin is not merely done and done with. The injury done in the soul remains in its effects. Even though Reuben was Jacob's most precious jewel in his treasury, Jacob disqualified him for the high position.

To understand the magnitude of Reuben's eventual demotion, the following lists the consequences that can remain within a family line for generations when carnal weaknesses are unconquered:

- Being prone to disloyalty, leading to divisiveness and rebellion. (*Numbers 16*)
- Being prone to spiritual and genetic weakness in leadership.
- Being prone to choose unwise actions, causing unnecessary reactions in others. (*Numbers 32; Joshua 22:10-20*)

- Being prone to complacency which divides the heart. (*Joshua 5:15-16*)
- Being prone to characteristic selfishness and innate fickleness. (*Judges 5:15-16*)
- Being easily captivated by the enemy's snares, detouring from the fulfillment of vision.

To combat these character flaws, it is important to be committed to overcoming areas of your life that do not reflect the qualities of leadership. In the following chapters we will take a deeper look into personal character development, examining the scriptural qualities that should be evident in the life of a man or woman of character.

Because of the prevalence of immorality in today's culture, we will also focus upon what it truly means to live a life of purity unto the Lord. What are the root causes of moral impurity? What does the Bible have to say about sexual sins? And how can a leader guard himself from falling into these sins?

Character development comes only with time, at great personal effort. May this book be an encouragement to you as you pursue a life of godly character.

Chapter Two

COMMITTED TO PERSONAL CHARACTER DEVELOPMENT

THE IMPORTANCE OF CHARACTER

*T*he Lord cares about a leader's lifestyle and character, not just his gifts and anointing. While the gifts of the Spirit are given freely, character development comes only with time, at great personal effort. This is why God invests time into His leaders, disciplining them, stretching them, and developing in them the character they need to become vessels of honor for His use. God knows that in order for there to be a long-lasting, effective ministry, it must be built upon character.

God doesn't care how long the character development will take, or how uncomfortable it will make a person feel, as long as there is growth. Today, God is committed to helping you develop the character that you will need to be an effective tool in his hand. Each Christian is responsible to partner with God in this life-long process.

> *"If I take care of my character,*
> *my reputation will take care of itself."*
> —D.L. MOODY

What begins in the heart must be carefully cultivated to full fruit in action. Heart qualities must be diligently pursued to pave the way for character development. God deals with His leaders to develop their character so that they may be vessels of honor for His use and effective in their ministries.

THE DEFINITION OF CHARACTER

If there must be a balance between gifts and character, what is character? The following descriptions display the different aspects of a definition of the word "character":

Character is the seat of one's moral being.

Character is the inner life of man. It will reflect either the traits of the sinful nature (being influenced by the world) or the traits of the divine nature (being influenced by the Word of God).

Character is displayed in the actions of an individual under pressure.

Finally, character is the sum total of all the negative and positive qualities in a person's life, exemplified by one's thoughts, values, motivations, attitudes, feelings, and actions.

"Talents are best nurtured in solitude. Character is best formed in the stormy billows of the world."

—JOHANN VON GOETHE

Greek Meanings

The Greek word for character offers much insight. In the King James Version, this Greek word, *charakter* is translated as "imagine." *Charakter,* a noun, is derived from the word *charasso,* which means a notch, indentation, a sharpening, scratching, or writing on stone. It came to mean the embossed stamp made on the coin or a character styled in writing.

This Greek word appears in the New Testament only in Hebrews 1:3. Here, the writer states that Christ is the very character of God, the very stamp of God's nature, and the one in whom God stamped or imprinted His being. Consequently, we derive the meaning of our English word "character" as a distinctive mark impressed, or otherwise formed, by an outside (or internal) force upon an individual.

MORE ABOUT CHARACTER

To help define what character is:

1. Character is what a person is at this present time. Character is not just what a person will ideally be in the future. When pressure comes to a person's life, the real person surfaces. A person may act and think one way under the blessings of the Lord, but quite another way when the trials of life are his portion.

2. Character includes a person's inner thoughts, motives, and attitudes, not just a person's actions. Thoughts, though hidden, indicate the real character of a person. Motives, too, are true expressions of the inner man. To change the character of a person, one must go deeper than action.

3. Character does not appear without pressure.
The pressures of life test what the Lord has really accomplished in a person's character. When the heat is upon a person's character, his true character surfaces. How do you respond to the disappointments and pressures of everyday life? The common irritations of everyday living expose the weaknesses in every person's life. Character is formed under such pressures and circumstances. The qualities that are truly part of a person's character are consistent, whether the heat is on or off his life.

4. Character is not only that which other people see on the external, but that which other people do not see. People may see only the side of a person that a person wants to display, but God sees the real person. An individual cannot hide his weaknesses from the Lord. Man may look at the external, but the Lord looks at the heart. The Lord commands good works from each one of us, but these must proceed out of a godly character. A person can do many outward religious works, and still be ungodly.

5. Character is not just having wisdom to comment on the behavior of others. Intellectually knowing how to act, think, and feel consistently with biblical principles may be a far cry from actually living in harmony with those principles. A person with true character doesn't just verbally tell other people what to do, but lives as an example worthy of following.

6. Character shows forth godly principles in every situation and toward all people. Character is not limited to relationships between Christians. To believe that it does not matter how a Christian acts toward non-Christians is a deception. For example, a Christian worker must give the same respect to an employer whether he is a Christian or not.

7. A person's character can be discerned by the way he respects and honors his mother and father. Character is not limited to a person's relationship with his spiritual family. It also shows in how he treats his natural family. A Christian must demonstrate his faith and love in the way he treats his immediate family. A Christian with an unbelieving natural family can win his family to Christ by having a mature, loving character toward them.

CHARACTER ASSESSMENT

What is a man of God? How do we recognize a spiritually mature person? What is God looking for in my leadership today? What specific qualities must I have to be a balanced leader? Am I a spiritual man?

As you honestly reflect through the following questions, you will be able to assess your own development of leadership character.

For Self-Evaluation

✓ Do I stay in close communion with the
   Holy Spirit?

✓ Do I accept the Bible as the Word of God?

✓ Do I love God's people?

✓ Do I identify with God's people in a specific local church?

✓ Do I willingly submit to authority?

✓ Do I love the sinner and the backslider?

✓ Do I truly worship God with all of my heart?

✓ Do I have a strong prayer life?

✓ Do I have a mature attitude in pressure situations?

✓ Do I let another person finish a job that I began without feeling any bitterness toward that person?

✓ Do I listen to and receive criticism?

✓ Do I accept it when someone else is assigned a job for which I am better qualified?

✓ Do I have inner peace during times of turmoil?

✓ Do I forgive someone who deliberately ignores me?

✓ Do I control my anger?

✓ Do I pass up certain present pleasures to achieve long term goals?

✓ Do I finish the projects that I begin?

✓ Do I put others before myself?

✓ Do I face unpleasant disappointments without any bitterness?

✓ Do I freely admit when I am wrong?

✓ Do I keep my promises and complete my commitments?

✓ Can I hold my tongue when it is best to do so?

✓ Do I accept and live in peace with the things I cannot change?

Even as the character of the world becomes more corrupt, the Lord is causing the character of the Church to be matured.

MAJOR CHARACTER AREAS

The Christian leader today must develop his character in these eight major areas of life in order to achieve God's goals for himself:

1. Spiritual life—A leader's relationship with the Lord is built upon a godly character as well as a depth of wisdom in God's Word and prayer.

2. Personal life—The habits, lifestyle and patterns which a leader develops will have a great influence upon the ministry he has received from the Lord.

3. Home life—A leader's personal family life will form the basis for his ministry to the family of God. A leader must first have his own home in order. This is based upon his character, for without character he will have no successful family life.

4. Social life—A leader's friendships reflect his character. A leader must develop character to have successful social relationships. Loyalty and acceptance are two great factors required in friendships. If a man has character, he will have the needed elements for a normal and good social life.

5. Educational life—Education by itself is not enough to build good character. But if character is developed through the disciplines of life, education can be a powerful force in the life of a leader. A good character enables a leader to receive a good education in and out of the classroom.

6. Ministerial life—Character is the very root of all that a governmental ministry does. Ministry function is, in itself, a manifestation of a leader's character. What he is will come out in what he does in his ministry. 1 Timothy 3 and Titus 1 list character qualifications as the basis for a leader's ministerial life.

7. Marital life—A leader's marital life will succeed only as he has a mature and developed character. A man without a developed character brings his deficiencies into the home with him. A leader's married life will blossom only if his character is cultivated; otherwise, he will never be able to meet the needs of his wife.

8. Financial life—Jesus Christ himself said that if a man did not know how to take care of money, God would not commit to him the true spiritual riches of the kingdom. A leader's frugality, wisdom, true desires, values, self-esteem, and ability to give are all demonstrated by how he uses the money that he has (though not necessarily by how much money he earns).

> *"Character, in great and little things, means carrying through what you feel able to do."*
> —JOHANN VON GOETHE

THE COST OF CHARACTER DEVELOPMENT

More than ever, the Christian needs to develop his character to resist being conformed into the different molds of this world. If the Church is to achieve and retain the image of the Lord Jesus, her leaders must lead the way. We need strong, godly character to stand against the attacks of the enemy. We need leaders who are willing to count the cost and pay the price of character development in their lives.

To count the cost is:

1. To consider one's goals and purpose in a realistic way.
2. To calculate how much energy and effort is needed to accomplish the whole task.
3. To anticipate distractions, hindrances, snares, and traps that will be in your path.
4. To list all the privileges you enjoy and then determine by careful analysis if these privileges will weaken your progression toward your goals. If they do, you must lay them aside.
5. To make a covenant with yourself that you will not give up in times of great discouragement, frustration or pressure.

CHARACTER ALL LEADERS MUST HAVE

6. To unite yourself with the kind of people who are going in the same direction.

7. To purpose in your spirit that you will accomplish God's purpose for your life in God's timing in God's way.

Encouragement from God for leaders who meet the challenge

→ I have not rejected you, but have chosen you. (Isaiah 41:8-9)

→ Fear not, I am with you. Be not dismayed. (Isaiah 41:10)

→ I am your God. (Isaiah 41:10)

→ I will strengthen you. (Isaiah 41:10)

→ I will uphold you with my victorious right hand. (Isaiah 41:10)

→ I will destroy all your enemies. (Isaiah 41:11-12)

→ I will make you a sharp threshing instrument. (Isaiah 41:15)

Chapter Three

THE CHARACTER
QUALIFICATIONS
OF LEADERSHIP

PAUL'S CHARACTER TESTS FOR LEADERSHIP

When Timothy stayed in Ephesus to support the apostle Paul and help the church mature, he often worked with men who wanted to be teachers and spiritual leaders in the church. In 1 Timothy 3:1, Paul commended those who wanted to lead by saying, "It is a fine work he desires."

Immediately after that, however, Paul gives a long list of qualifications. Obviously, he wanted Timothy to select a certain kind of man to be a church leader. Paul's teaching to Timothy and Titus forms a powerful profile for testing a Christian's maturity level.

A man of God does not "suddenly appear." He is cultivated by the Holy Spirit in a slow process. Timothy in Ephesus, and Titus on the island of Crete, had to test many who aspired to leadership. Paul's letters to them provided the character tests for leadership, which are a yardstick for measuring Christian character development in general.

In 1 Timothy 3:1-13 and Titus 1:5-9, the standards of character maturity are many.

Above Reproach

(1 Timothy 3:2, Titus 1:7)

Blameless, having unquestionable integrity, irreproachable—"not to be taken hold of," having such character that no one can rightfully take hold of the person with a charge of wrongdoing. Therefore, an elder* must be an example to the flock of God, and free from the taint of scandal and accusation. An elder must conduct himself so well that any accusation is rendered absurd and unfounded from the outset.

A person above reproach is:

"One that cannot be called to account, unreprovable or unaccused" (1 Timothy 3:2, Thayer)

"One that gives no ground for accusation" (3:2, AMP)

"Of blameless reputation" (Titus 1:7, Philips)

"Of unquestionable integrity and irreproachable" (1:7, AMP)

---

* While these qualifications were for selecting elders, all Christian leaders should seek to acquire these character qualities.

Husband of One Wife

(1 Timothy 3:2; Titus 1:6)

This does not mean that an elder must be married (Paul was not), but that, if married, he should be married to one wife.

A husband of one wife is:

Not a bigamist

"One wife's husband" (Lenski)

As "one wife's husband," a man has nothing to do with any other woman. He must be a man who cannot be accused on the score of sexual promiscuity or laxity. At different times and in different churches, "one husband's wife" has had spiritual meanings as well.

To the Roman Catholic Church, the bishop's one wife is the Church, to whom he must remain faithful. Some European churches prohibit widowers who have remarried from serving as bishops. Early

Church fathers allowed a man already married to be ordained, but if he was single when ordained, he must remain so all of his life. Some Church leaders maintain that any record of divorce, even if before conversion, would disqualify a man from taking office.

The morals and social environment of Paul's day certainly made this character standard an important one. Pagan temple prostitutes were used regularly by man, without social stigma. "Companion" girls were often used by both married and unmarried men. Many men openly kept mistresses.

But in requiring leaders to be "the husband of one wife," Paul required them to be intimately related to only one woman. And Jesus Himself had earlier set an even higher standard: he who "looks on a woman to lust" (greatly desires for a sexual, physical relation- ship) is guilty of sin. Note, however, that this standard differentiates temptation, with much less personal involvement, from the sin of lust.

In the environment of Paul's day, a happily married man handled the many available sexual temptations better than the man with a bad marriage. Paul is thus saying that a leader must have a strong marriage, with a healthy sex life, and must not deliberately expose himself to sexual temptations (such as today's pornographic magazines). A man and woman must work hard to cultivate a tremendous unity and love in their marriage. A man should never share his private struggles with another woman, only with his wife or mature men of God. Single men should never share their struggles with other single women, and sometimes not with some single men, either.

Temperate

(1 Timothy 3:2; Titus 1:8)

This character quality denotes keeping oneself in hand, self-controlled, and disciplined. An elder must be able to control (rule) himself in all respects:

"Self-controlled over appetite and affection" (Concordant Literal)

"A man who is discreet" (Titus 1:8, Phillips)

Free from extremes

Having power over or control of a thing (Robertson)

Some related meanings are worth developing. The exhortation to be sober (1 Thessalonians 5:6,8) is a call to temperance. In 2 Timothy 4:5, Paul exhorts Timothy to "Endure... do the work... make full proof." A temperate man has a clean perspective on life, and a correct and fruitful spiritual orientation. A temperate man does not lose his physical, psychological, or spiritual balance. He is stable, steadfast, always thinking clearly, and doesn't lose his perspective under pressure. He does not get caught up in false security of the day; he has a proper perspective.

Prudent

(1 Timothy 3:2)

This is to be sober-minded, prudent, sensible; not given to fanciful thinking or emotional irrationality; using sound judgment.

A prudent person is:

"Fair-minded" (1 Tim. 3:2, Phillips)

"Disciplined" (Titus 1:8)

So many religious fads, fancies, and unstable ways are offered to leaders today. Leaders with a safe, sane steady mind in all matters of life will not be easily shaken from God's path.

Dictionary definitions of "prudent" commonly include these elements: cautious, having practical wisdom, exercising carefulness over the consequences of actions, and being able to foresee the future through understanding the present.

In Proverbs, a prudent man "covereth shame" and "looketh well to his ways"; he "responds to correction" and is "hungry for training." See Proverbs 12:16,23 and 13:16 and 14:8,15,18 and 15:5 and 16:21 and 18:15 and 19:14 and 22:3 and 27:12.

Respectable

(1 Timothy 3:2)

Of good behavior, having a modest, orderly, disciplined, respectable lifestyle.

A respectable person is:

Orderly or moderate

Not light or vain

Has a composure that brings no reproach upon the ministry of the Lord.

The Greek word for "respectable" should be understood in its broadest sense as denoting a character quality, and goes well beyond a refined, courteous, polite person. A respectable man lives a well-ordered life. The verb form of "respectable" in Greek is *kosmeo*. It is used to describe a well-ordered house (Matthew 12:44), a decorated tombstone (Matthew 23:29) and well-trimmed lamps (Matthew 25:7).

Paul is saying here that a man who is respectable has a lifestyle that adorns the teachings of the Bible in his speech, his dress, his appearance at home, his office, or the way he does business. God is a God of order. A man of God, too, should be orderly and proper. (Other scriptures: 1 Thessalonians 4:10-12; Colossians 3:23,24; 1 Timothy 6:2; Colossians 4:5,6; 1 Peter 2:12; Philippians 1:27).

Hospitable

(1 Timothy 3:2; Titus 1:6)

Quite simply, this means "fond of guests"

(strangers). It means more than simply taking people into your home. It means being fond of and kind to them while they are there. An elder must enjoy having guests in his home and being a help to strangers.

Fond of guests; enjoys the company of others, especially believers (1 Timothy 3:2).

Loving and a friend to believers, strangers, and foreigners (Titus 1:6 AMP).

"(If the) stranger resides in your home, do him no wrong... (he) shall be as your native among you, love him as yourself" (Leviticus 19:33,34).

"Let love of brethren continue...do not neglect to show hospitality" (Hebrews 13:1,2).

"Be hospitable to one another without complaining" (1 Peter 4:9).

Apt to Teach

(1 Timothy 3:2)

That is, a skilled teacher. The Greek word does not mean simply to teach, it means to teach in a skillful manner.

"Instructive or able to communicate"
(1 Timothy 3:2).

Able to teach, resulting from having been taught.

Implied as having the ability to prove the critic and unbeliever wrong, with the result being a proper communication of the truth of God's Word (Titus 1:9).

The Greek word used here *didakitkos* means able to impart truth. It could also be translated as "teachable." It refers to a quality of life: humble, sensitive, desirous to know the will of God.

One who is *didakitkos* does not look for arguments or stir them up. He is sensitive to people, even those who are confused, obstinate, and bitter. When verbally or even physically attacked, he does not reciprocate with cutting words and putdowns. This is a self-controlled lifestyle.

Those who are apt to teach are also apt to learn. They learn more of the Word (2 Timothy 2:2). They progressively believe more of the Word (Titus 1:9). And they progressively live more of the Word (2 Timothy 2:24,25).

Not Given to Wine

(1 Tim. 3:3; Titus 1:7; Proverbs 20:1)

Literally, not tarrying at wine or staying near wine.

"One who sits long at his wine" (Robertson).

One who drinks alcoholic beverages often and in large amounts.

Would Paul condone drinking at all? In this passage, he is not speaking of total abstinence. He uses a word, *paoinos* that definitely refers to excess, meaning that he is talking about the kind of drinking that causes one to lose control of his senses and be brought into bondage. Paul here is talking about overdrinking. And the consequences of this are indeed terrible (Proverbs 23:29-34). A higher law rules us in this matter: we should not do "anything by which your brother stumbles" (Romans 14:21).

Not Self-willed

(Titus 1:7)

An elder must not be dominated by self-interest, stubbornness, or arrogance. He must submit to proper authority, seek to please God and others, and not become "set" in his ways.

Not insubordinate

"Not stubborn" (Williams)

"Not given to self-gratification" (Concordant Literal)

"Arrogant or presumptuous" (AMP)

"Self-centered and wants to do as he pleases" (Beck)

"Self-pleasing and arrogant" (Thayer)

A self-willed person is set on having his own way, never seems to lay down his desires in order to serve another, and when he finally does, he does it grudgingly. The self-willed man builds the world around himself. The self-willed man is his own authority! (2 Peter 2:2, 3,10,14,18)

That probably couldn't describe any of us reading this book. But just to be sure, ask yourself these questions:

Do you usually or always get your way?

Do you have difficulty admitting your mistakes?

Do you rule your own home with authoritarian leadership — "Do it because I told you to do it"?

As a child, were you overindulged, and did you have problems with being conceited or spoiled?

Self-will and strong-willed are two different things. The spiritually mature person will not dominate others, even if he does have a strong will.

Not Quick-Tempered

(Titus 1:7)

Not soon angry, not prone to anger or quick-tempered. An elder must not be irascible, cranky or irritable.

CHARACTER ALL LEADERS MUST HAVE

Not easily provoked or inflamed

"Not quick-tempered" (Titus 1:7 AMP)

"Capable of governing your own spirit"
(Kevin J. Conner)

The person who is not easily angered doesn't
have a "short fuse" or "fly off the handle." Our
guide in dealing with anger is Ephesians 4:26, "Be
angry, and sin not." Some feelings of anger are
inevitable in this fallen world. But if we quickly
release and forsake them, they will not harm us.
Brooding anger hurts the spirit; smoldering,
revenge-seeking anger causes a man to lose perspective. Those who are "slow to anger" (James
1:19,20) will find it much easier to cooperate with
the moving of the Holy Spirit.

Not Pugnacious

(1 Timothy 3:3; Titus 1:7)

Not violent, combative or pugnacious. A pugnacious man carries a chip on his shoulder and is always ready for a good argument, perhaps even just a good theological tussle!

Not quarrelsome

Not disposed to arguments or fighting

A pugnacious person loses control of his senses and is controlled by anger. He is always ready to fight, with a combative, belligerent nature. He can't avoid engaging in physical violence.

Be comforted in this fact: God has helped and used some people who had a problem with anger. Moses had a history of anger. He killed an Egyptian (Acts 7:20-29); he threw down and broke the Tablets of the Law which God gave him; he angrily smote

God's rock of provision in the wilderness, contrary to God's command (Numbers 20:1-13). In spite of all this, the Lord used Moses in a mighty way. Peter also was rash in word and deed; he cut off the ear of the high priest's servant on the night of Christ's arrest (John 18:1-27).

Not contentious

(1 Timothy 3:3)

Not contentious, not a brawler. This signifies someone who is not quarrelsome and contentious, but is peaceable. An elder must be a man of peace.

"Not to be withstood; invincible" (Thayer)

Peaceable

(1 Tim. 3:3)

Easily corrected

The contentious person domineers others, but in reality is insecure and defensive. He struggles against others, and has to compete with and debate others. He is not happy unless he is in charge, and not willing to serve or come under anyone else. He is not willing to bend, not flexible: "It's my way or no way!" Such people, usually jealous and selfish, are motivated by pride. He is apt to contend and argue, and loves controversy, strife, conflict, struggle and discord.

By contrast, a Christian leader has the character quality of being one who seeks peace. "With all that lies within you...live at peace with one another" is his motto (Romans 12:16,18). This person is easily corrected.

Gentle

(1 Timothy 3:2)

Patient; that is, gentle, kind, considerate, and forbearing.

A gentle person:

Has a mild disposition.

Is gentle or considerate (Robertson).

In Philippians 4:5, this same word is translated in various versions as "moderation," "forbearance," and "sweet reasonableness." This Greek word, *epiekes* means "trench," and, by extension, "yielding." It is used in the context of not insisting on one's legal rights; legal rights can become moral wrongs when a person takes advantage or has the upper hand on someone else too often.

In a noble and generous spirit, a superior person will even yield to the lesser. Galatians 6:1 tells us to restore people "in a spirit of gentleness."

Free from Love of Money

(1 Timothy 3:3)

This person is not greedy for money. Basically one word in the Greek, it means not acquiring money by dishonest means or acquiring dishonest money by any means. This person is:

Not fond of money (Concordant Literal)

Not pursuing dishonest gain (1 Tim. 3:3, NIV)

Free from the love of money (Titus 1:7)

This person is not covetous of other possessions as well. He is not a lover of (fond of) money, not avaricious, and simply "not greedy." An elder must be free from the love of money and the things it can obtain. Being insatiable for wealth and ready to obtain it (1 Timothy 3:3 AMP) by questionable means obviously disqualifies someone from Christian leadership. It renders spiritual growth impossible.

Rules His Own House Well

(1 Timothy 3:4; Titus 1:6)

An elder must preside over and manage his own household (family members, finances, possessions, etc.) in an excellent manner. The ruling aspect includes the concept of concerned (caring) management. This requires more than just watching the overall direction, but also requires helping to conduct the affairs of the family. The word "well" in the Greek is a strong term, meaning beautiful or excellent, as opposed to just pretty or fair.

"Children in subjection with all gravity" is holding or keeping children under control (in obedience, submission). The term "all gravity" could apply to the elder or to his children or both. "All gravity" means true dignity, respect, and reverence. "Faithful children" refers to "believing children," or children who believe in Jesus Christ as their Savior (that is, they are Christians). Elders' children are to be Christians.

Children in Subjection

(1 Tim. 3:4)

Controlling his own household (Concordant Literal)

Whose children are well-trained and are believers, not open to accusation of being loose in morals and conduct or unruly and disorderly (Titus 1:6 AMP).

This passage does not speak of very small children. These little ones will go through phases of difficulty, but if there is not willful, loose living, time will tell if the parents trained well. "Dissipated rebellion" could only speak of older children who have reached the age of accountability. Riotous and improper living is characteristic of the common rebellion among older teenagers and young adults. In I Samuel 2:12, the two sons of Eli are disqualified from the priesthood because their riotous living made them *"sons of Belial"* (2:17). To truly love our spouses and children, we must discipline them in love (Ephesians 5:25; 1 Peter 3:7).

A Good Reputation with Those Outside the Church

(1 Timothy 3:7)

This is the result of living an excellent testimony for those outside of the church (the non-Christian community). A reputation may exist in areas of business, community relations, and civil law. An elder must be a respected person "on the job" as well as in the church.

An example of Christian virtue in the community in regard to integrity, honesty, and purity:

"Behave properly toward outsiders"
(1 Thessalonians 4:11,12)

"Conduct yourself with wisdom toward the outsiders" (Colossians 4:3,6)

"Give none offense, neither to the Jews, nor to the Gentiles" (1 Corinthians 10:31-33)

"Having your conversation honest among the Gentiles" (1 Peter 2:12)

Lover of Good

(Titus 1:8)

Although the King James Version has "lover of good men," the Greek word here is much broader than that. It means being fond of good—good men, good activities, things, thoughts, etc. An elder's desires should be toward the good things of God, and not set on evil, questionable or less important things.

"One who loves good things and good people" (Titus 1:8 AMP)

"One who loves what is good" (Titus 1:8 NIV)

A Promoter of Virtue

This mindset is described in detail in Philippians 4:8, which lists many good things for the believer to dwell on: "whatsoever things are true... honest... just... pure... lovely... of good report... any virtue... any praise."

Just

(Titus 1:8)

That is, righteous, equitable, and upright. This entails not only right standing before God, but also doing what is right and just in one's dealings with other people. It is conduct that meets the approval of the divine Judge.

The just man is:

Equitable in character

Fair in decisions (Titus 1:8)

Right in judgment

Upright and fair-minded

The just man can make mature decisions and proper judgments. God blessed Solomon exceedingly because, rather than asking for wealth, he prayed this prayer: "Lord, give me an understanding heart." Other examples of just men: Joseph (Matthew 1:19); Cornelius (Acts 10:22); John the Baptist (Mark 6:20).

Devout

(Titus 1:8)

A devout man pursues holiness, pleases God, and is set apart for His service. The opposite of this character quality is worldliness and carnality.

"Essential nature and character in relationship to God" (Kevin J. Conner)

Benign (Concordant Literal)

A devout man and religiously right (Titus 1:8
AMP)

A devout man actively and consistently practices
righteousness. He maintains his moral and religious
obligations.

Not a Novice

(1 Timothy 3:6)

That is, not a newly-converted Christian.

Not a new convert (1 Tim. 3:6 AMP)

"One who is newly planted" (Robertson)

Hopeful beginners who have ministry qualifications still lack the maturity in the faith that is
needed. This refers not to a young man's age, but to
his spiritual maturity.

Such a leader can easily become "conceited," which in the Greek means to wrap in smoke, or "besmoked" pride that covers him like a fog. In this fogged position, the devil can easily make him stumble.

In America, the Church quickly elevates to spiritual leadership newly-saved television and cinema stars, and "chief sinners," almost immediately after their conversion. This violates the Bible command in 1 Timothy 3:6. Some of these "hothouse growth" leaders survive this mistake, some are ruined for life, and others never seem to find a balanced role in ministry.

Holds Fast the Faithful Word

(Titus 1:9)

An elder must have a firm grip and a strong hold on the Word of God as it was taught to him. He must know the Scriptures and the proper teaching (sound doctrine) he received. See also 2 Timothy 2:2.

Holding fast the faithful Word involves:

"Never being willing to compromise truth" (Kevin J. Conner)

A deep conviction of the infallibility and authority of Scripture

Not Double-Tongued

(1 Timothy 3:8)
This involves:

Not being shifty or a double-talker, but being sincere in what you say (1 Timothy 3:8)

Not standing between two persons, saying something to one person, and then saying the complete opposite to the other.

CHOOSING CO-LABORERS

The following list identifies some of the most important character qualities that a shepherd should look for when he chooses co-laborers:

- Integrity
- Sharing the same spirit and burden
- Faithfulness
- Commitment to the church
- Right attitudes
- A shepherd's heart
- Stability
- An ability to get along with people
- Deliberation in making decisions
- A lover and enjoyer of other people
- Not domineering
- Gracious
- Not a respecter of people
- A servant's heart

- Not a busybody
- Guards a secret
- A spirit of sacrifice
- Successful in a secular job
- Lives consistently with biblical principles
- Not addicted to the gods of this world
- Good habits
- Doer of the Word
- Teachable spirit
- Love for God's House
- Receives correction and changes
- Supportive, not competitive toward others
- Submissive spirit
- Humble heart
- Transparent, open and honest nature

May every leader strive to develop these attitudes and qualities in his own life, allowing the Lord to mold him into the image of His dear son, Jesus Christ.

Chapter Four

LIVING A LIFE
OF MORAL PURITY

The minister most likely to stray into moral impurity is not much different from men in other professions who stray. Research shows he usually is middle-aged and disillusioned with his calling. He has neglected his own marriage and has met another woman who needs him. He is a lone ranger, isolated from his clerical peers. However, his association with God makes his moral failure more serious than immorality among other professionals. The public sees his authority as derived from the Lord, setting him apart even from other so-called professional counselors or therapists.

The Reverend Henry Ward Beecher, the great preacher of the late nineteenth century, was nearly ruined after an illicit affair became known. In the late twentieth century several prominent leaders in the Christian world fell into moral impurity. It occurs in all denominations. Pentecostals fall alongside evangelicals. During rousing rituals, a minister can appear to command great power. One counselor-therapist who works to restore fallen ministries says this power is closely linked to sexual passion. Women may imagine a tremendous benefit in sexual union with the minister, while nearsighted ministers block out thoughts of judgment as they indulge their flesh and fantasies.

Moral impurity is like an infection. An infection puts poison into a healthy body and causes disease. It taints and corrupts. It is a malfunction or sickness that, if not remedied, leads to death. Biblical prescriptions can treat immorality. A diagnosis locates infected areas that need treatment. The prescription for treatment calls for cleansing and proper remedies. Good health depends on good diagnoses and good medicines.

Perversion and filthiness surround people today like it surrounded Lot. Lot lived in a corrupt society vexed by unrestrained evil and moral impurity. It was filthy.

2 PETER 2:6-9

If he condemned the cities of Sodom and Gomorrah by burning them to ashes, and made them an example of what is going to happen to the ungodly; and if he rescued Lot, a righteous man, who was distressed by the filthy lives of lawless men (for that righteous man, living among them day after day, was tormented in his righteous soul by the lawless deeds he saw and heard)—if this is so, then the Lord knows how to rescue godly men from trials and to hold the unrighteous for the day of judgment, while continuing their punishment. (NIV)

A righteous man purifies his soul and removes filth that causes infection. The Hebrew word for *filth* means stained, dirty, abominable, unclean, and foul. It describes anything that soils or defiles. The Greek word for *filth* means to stain, soil, or smear. It refers especially to sexual or sensual defilements. The word *defile* means to discolor something by painting or staining it, making it unclean. The following verses warn and encourage believers, including leaders, to avoid filth, defilement, and corruption.

ISAIAH 4:4

The Lord will wash away the filth of the women of Zion; he will cleanse the bloodstains from Jerusalem by a spirit of judgment and a spirit of fire. (NIV)

JAMES 1:21

Therefore, get rid of all moral filth and the evil that is so prevalent and humbly accept the word planted in you, which can save you. (NIV)

PROVERBS 30:12

There are those who are pure in their own eyes and yet are not cleansed of their filth. (NIV)

2 CORINTHIANS 7:1

Since we have these promises, dear friends, let us purify ourselves from everything that contaminates body and spirit, perfecting holiness out of reverence for God. (NIV)

Joshua is told to remove his filthy garments in Zechariah 3:3-4, and Colossians 3:8 tells Christians to put off all uncleanness. Impurity and sexual misconduct pave the way for future rebellion and disobedience. Societies that fail to restrain moral impurity also run wild with rebellion and disrespect for authority.

Second Peter 2:10 talks of those who walk according to the flesh in the lust of uncleanness and despise authority. They are presumptuous and self-willed. They are not afraid to speak evil of dignitaries.

SEVEN ROOT CAUSES OF MORAL IMPURITY

Western society has been infected with moral impurity and now suffers the full-blown disease. Its symptoms include pagan morals and values held by the general public. The symptoms point to the following root causes of spiritual infections:

1. Failing to cleanse oneself of daily sins— Salvation cleanses man's heart or his inner man. He is responsible to keep his heart clean by walking in the light and applying the blood of Jesus to his daily sins (see I John 1:7-9; Ps. 51:10,17; 139:23; Prov. 4:23; 15:28; Matt. 5:8; 2 Tim. 2:12).

EZEKIEL 36:25-27

> I will sprinkle clean water on you, and you
> will be clean; I will cleanse you from all your
> impurities and from all your idols. I will give
> you a new heart and put a new spirit in you;
> I will remove from you your heart of stone
> and give you a heart of flesh. And I will put
> my Spirit in you and move you to follow my
> decrees and be careful to keep my laws. (NIV)

2. Secret sins—Secret sins are hidden, covered, veiled, concealed, or disguised. When God exposes secret sins, he allows others to see sin's devastating consequences.

PSALM 19:12

Who can discern his errors? Forgive my hidden faults. (NIV)

PROVERBS 28:13

He who conceals his sins does not prosper, but whoever confesses and renounces them finds mercy. (NIV)

Crafty characters glamorize the pleasures of sin and tempt believers to think like the foolish man in Proverbs. He thought the pleasures of sin would last a long time. They don't. The believer should hate sin, knowing it undercuts his potential and blocks his achievement of what God has planned for him. He should hate sin as he sees it damaging the lives of people he loves. However, he will not hate sin if he does not comprehend its final cost. Unconfessed sin will cause uncontrolled miseries (Matt. 10:26-27).

PSALM 51:6

Surely you desire truth in the inner parts; you teach me wisdom in the inmost place. (NIV)

1 CORINTHIANS 3:13

His work will be shown for what it is, because the Day will bring it to light. It will be revealed with fire, and the fire will test the quality of each man's work. (NIV)

Scripture is clear. God's remedy for man's sin is confession. God will reveal hidden things, and man is responsible to confess and forsake them. God gives every man time to repent (Rev. 2:21). It is just a matter of time until a man's sin is revealed. If he repents first, God may be the only one to see the consequences of the sin. If not, the consequences may be seen by all.

3. Impure thinking—Christians must not only seek heaven but also think of heaven. They need to expose every thought to God and his Word.

COLOSSIANS 3:2

> Set your minds on things above, not on earthly things. (NIV)

Evil thinking leads to evil desires. Evil desires lead to evil actions, which ultimately become enslaving habits. To set an example for others, a leader needs to immediately cleanse wrong thoughts so they do not destroy his emotions or affections. He needs to turn every one of his thoughts into discussions with God so that God can have His rightful place in the leader's thoughts and cleanse them by Holy Spirit conviction. A man can rebuild his thinking through memorizing and meditating on Scripture.

COLOSSIANS 3:3-5

> For you died, and your life is now hidden with Christ in God. When Christ, who is your life, appears, then you also will appear with him in

glory. Put to death, therefore, whatever belongs to your earthly nature: sexual immorality, impurity, lust, evil desires, and greed, which is idolatry. (NIV)

Exploiters and manipulators know the basic instincts of man. They know how to exploit the minds of other men to make them lust after ungodly things and enslave them. Stories and advertisements in broadcast and print media engulf the populace with messages aimed at men's basic desires.

4. Defiling habits–A habit is part of a person's lifestyle or his habitation—the place he lives. Frequent repetition of an act makes it a habit.

ROMANS 13:14

Rather, clothe yourselves with the Lord Jesus Christ, and do not think about how to gratify the desires of the sinful nature. (NIV)

A person is a slave to whatever he submits to. The apostle Paul exhorts Christians not to present their bodies as instruments of sin, not to let sin reign, and not to obey sin's lusts (Rom. 6:12-14). Believers need to walk in the power of the Holy Spirit and in holiness to make their habits holy unto the Lord.

5. Modern-day idolatry—Idolatry is an excessive attachment to or love for something or someone besides God. It has to do with an individual's heart, emotions, and talents. Giving prime time and attention to anything other than God makes a man an unholy idolater. Using resources that God has provided in ways that do not glorify God is a form of idolatry.

1 CORINTHIANS 10:7

> Do not be idolaters, as some of them were; as it is written: "The people sat down to eat and drink and got up to indulge in pagan revelry." (NIV)

I JOHN 5:21

Dear children, keep yourselves from idols. (NIV)

LEVITICUS 26:1

Do not make idols or set up an image or a sacred stone for yourselves, and do not place a carved stone in your land to bow down before it. I am the LORD your God. (NIV)

COLOSSIANS 3:5

Put to death... sexual immorality, impurity, lust, evil desires and greed, which is idolatry. (NIV)

6. Defiled conscience—Sensitive to moral pleasure and pain, the conscience can be called man's inner umpire. It distinguishes between right and wrong. It dwells in the spirit of a man, urging him to do right and warning him to steer clear of wrong. A clear conscience is essential for success in spiritual warfare. Ignorance of how the conscience does its job can lead to serious spiritual disorders (1 Cor. 1:12; 1 Tim 3:9; 2 Tim 1:3; Heb.13:18).

ACTS 24:16

So I strive always to keep my conscience clear before God and man. (NIV)

1 TIMOTHY 1:5,19

The goal of this command is love, which comes from a pure heart and a good conscience and a sincere faith.... Holding on to faith and a good conscience. Some have rejected these and so have shipwrecked their faith. (NIV)

Man is comprised of body, soul, and spirit. The body houses the five natural senses of smell, sight, hearing, touch, and taste. The soul includes a person's mind, will, and emotions. The spirit is home to a man's intuition and conscience. The conscience is the nerve center of the inner man. It judges the moral quality of a man's decisions and actions. It approves and disapproves his decisions and helps him regulate his choices and wishes.

The conscience is a unique, innate faculty put into human beings to hear the voice of God. God created it to guide people to make choices that please Him. If defiled, it becomes unreliable. However, a defiled conscience can be purged and retrained by the Holy Spirit to keep believers on the right track. The conscience is not the supernatural voice of God. A man's conscience delivers a judgment, but his will decides whether to act. When regulated by the Word of God, the conscience grows strong and insists on doing right, condemns wrongdoing, causes remorse over sin, and rewards righteousness with peace.

When not regulated by the Word of God, the conscience grows weak and may become defiled.

Defilement speaks of moral corruption in the soul
(1 Cor. 8:7,10,12).

> To the pure, all things are pure, but to those
> who are corrupted and do not believe,
> nothing is pure. In fact, both their minds and
> consciences are corrupted. (NIV)

Some people's consciences may never have been
strengthened by the Word of God. Some may be
weak because of incomplete knowledge of God's
will revealed in the Bible. Some may be weak due to
unsurrendered wills. And some that were strong
may grow weak by ignoring the Word of God. A conscience left in this state of weakness and defilement
may become hardened or seared.

God's Word is truth. If a man's actions do not
line up with the truth, he lives in deception.
When he resists the conviction of the Holy Spirit,

rationalizes and excuses his actions, and tries to hide from God, he defiles his conscience. Repeated violation of God's Word produces greater defilement until the man's conscience withers. Lowering his standards continually puts him in bondage to his secret sin.

1 TIMOTHY 4:2

>...speaking lies in hypocrisy, having their own conscience seared with a hot iron. (NKJV)

The word "seared" means utterly insensitive or withered up. It describes a plant wilting in the heat. Evil practiced habitually makes a man's conscience insensitive. Repeatedly defiled, it voices no resistance.

God designed guilt to lead people to repentance, not to despair. The Holy Spirit works in man's conscience to make him aware of his guilt. Every violation triggers immediate guilt, which should not be ignored. Man finds help only when he faces reality, admits guilt, and repents. When a man tries to blameshift or punish himself, he handles guilt the wrong way. Handling guilt improperly brings no cleansing and further weakens his conscience.

A defiled conscience can change a man's personality. It can make him defensive or depressed. It can make him double-minded and unstable in all his ways, causing him to vacillate on every decision. A defiled conscience often makes a man talkative, nervous, and unable to concentrate. It can drive away his friends. He must ask the Holy Spirit to apply the blood of Jesus to cover the sin and cleanse his conscience (Heb. 9:9-14). In response to a man's faith, the Holy Spirit applies the power of the blood of Christ to his conscience.

Let us draw near with a true heart in full assurance of faith, having our hearts sprinkled from an evil conscience and our bodies washed with pure water (Heb. 10:22, NKJV).

The sacrifice of the red heifer, spoken of in Hebrews 9:15 and alluded to in Hebrews 10:22, always was available and accessible. It could be offered at any time to cleanse violators of the law. God looks for the sinner to respond to conviction like King David. When confronted with his sin, David quickly said, "I have sinned against the Lord" (II Samuel 12:13).

To live in moral purity, a man must restore his conscience. Memorizing portions of Scripture will allow a fresh flow of the Holy Spirit to cleanse his mind and strengthen his conscience. The Scripture gives him God's thoughts to apply in areas of weakness. He can keep his conscience clear by limiting his daily exposure to known temptations. With the removal of the dead weight of past sin, his soul will soar like a lark with a song, released in its native element. The Holy Spirit delights to help men live free of offense toward God and man.

7. Absence of moral standards—Moral standards influence a person's attitude toward God and toward life. Unfortunately, what people say and what they do are miles apart. The land is full of adulterers, and the truth of Jeremiah 23:9-17 is being fulfilled in our lifetime. Sex saturates society. Fidelity is out, and adultery is in. Books, magazines, billboards, and movies promote it ceaselessly. Soap operas and talk shows continually send the message, "Sex is good in or out of marriage. Get all you can, any time you can." A prominent sexologist recommends "healthy adultery" for couples, arguing that it rejuvenates romance.

Immorality in society threatens church purity. Permissive attitudes tend to infiltrate the church. Some Christian leaders act as if anything goes. Love covers all. They accept everything. They don't preach against immorality in the church body. They don't mention the word *adultery*. They don't emphasize the holiness and purity of God.

In the past thirty or forty years, some church leaders have loosened their standards hoping to make the church relevant to society. However, their efforts to make their churches so relevant have instead made them irrelevant.

TODAY'S CHURCHES FOUND WANTING

There is a school of thought which says the solution to America's worst ills—rising violence accompanied by a total lack of conscience among criminals, unwed mothers and infant mortality, poverty and drugs—is a return to religion. For sickness of the soul, nothing less than a spiritual cure will do. But what if the churches aren't there to go back to?

The unbelieving world mocks Christians who compromise biblical standards. When a church leader lowers his standards to improve his image in the public eye or to be seen as "in touch" with the philosophies of the day, he actually destroys the distinctives of the church. He destroys the essence of his own ministry.

Leaders must draw lines. They must exalt the faithful, consistent standards of the Word of God, and those standards forbid moral impurity. It cannot be swept under the carpet or ignored. It will be judged by God. Fallen leaders must repent of it. Leaders must lift their voices like trumpets and declare that premarital sex and adultery are wrong.

UNDERSTANDING THE WRATH OF GOD

People need to see that immorality in the church and in the world draws the wrath of God. The wrath of God is not fiction or a figure of speech but is a terrible reality. It is the constant, unchanging reaction of God's holiness and righteousness to sin. It is not a passion for revenge or just a display of anger as human wrath tends to be. Within the framework of covenant theology, the wrath of God is an expression of rejected and wounded love. God has the last word when man indulges in human perversion. Man cannot escape. God's wrath is revealed (Rev. 6:16; Ps. 76:7).

For the wrath of God is revealed from heaven against all ungodliness and unrighteousness of men, who suppress the truth in unrighteousness. (Romans 1:18, NKJV).

Let no one deceive you with empty words, for because of these things the wrath of God comes upon the sons of disobedience (Ephesians 5:6, NKJV).

God judges the righteous, and God is angry with the wicked every day (Psalm 7:11). God's wrath has fallen on society because impurity has become a way of life. Society has indulged in almost every form of sexual immorality mentioned in the Bible, and people have become callous to guilt.

SEXUAL SIN

The Bible uses the following words to define sexual immorality:

Sensuality is a planned appeal to the physical senses for personal gratification. It is a preoccupation with bodily or sexual pleasure. It means to be governed by appetites and passions of the flesh (1 Cor. 2:14; James 3:15; Jude 19).

Lasciviousness is a tendency to excite sexual desires that cannot be righteously fulfilled. It refers to unbridled lust, shameless, filthy words, and indecent bodily movements (Mark 7:22; Rom. 13:13; 2 Cor. 12:21; Gal. 5:19; Eph. 4:19; 1 Pet. 4:3; 2 Pet. 2:7,18; Jude 19).

Fleshly lusts are strong cravings, longings, or desires for what is forbidden. People with fleshly lusts have strong, abnormal sexual desires or appetites.

To *defraud* means to obtain something from a person by deception. It means to take advantage, overreach, cheat, deceive (2 Cor. 2:11; 7:2; 12:17-18; 1 Thess. 4:6).

Fornication is sex outside of marriage or voluntary sexual acts between an unmarried man and woman. Fornicators prostitute their bodies outside of a marriage covenant (1 Cor. 6:13, 18; 1 Thess. 4:3; Heb. 12:16).

Adultery is sex between a married person and a partner other than his or her spouse (Ex. 20:14; Heb. 13:4).

Homosexuality is sexual intercourse between two people of the same sex. The Bible rejects it as an acceptable lifestyle because it perverts God's natural order for sexual identity and fulfillment. Today, the issue of homosexuality has become a source of division, even within the Church, because of how God's Word on this issue is interpreted. James 1:17 tells us, however, that God does not change "like shifting shadows" (NIV). His Word remains true throughout the ages, and His Word contains many references to the sin of homosexuality. In Genesis 19, the wickedness of the men of those cities brought divine destruction. In Leviticus 18:22 and 24, homosexuality is described as an "abomination" and "defiling." And in Romans 1:18-32, the Apostle Paul talked about this sin using the following terms: "unclean," "dishonorable," "vile," "unseemly," "wicked," "unrighteous," and "against nature."

People who have committed immoral acts often demonstrate telltale signs. They frequently appear argumentative, resentful, and nervous. They reject standards from the Word of God, wear provocative clothes, and redefine their moral convictions. They may lie, drop close friends, and avoid getting near people. They may not be able to engage in normal conversations. Moral bondage exists when human desires conflict with God's nature, but moral freedom reigns when God's desires become our desires.

STAGES OF ADULTERY

Like other men, godly leaders must deal with temptations to commit adultery. Even Elijah was a man "with a nature like ours" (James 4:17) and had to contend with temptations "common to man" (1 Corinthians 10:13). The Bible says, "Thou shalt not commit adultery" (Exodus 20:14), and adulterers in the Old Testament fell under the death penalty (Leviticus 20:10).

Adultery slips quietly into a person's life. Men and women do not usually wake up one morning and decide it's a good day to commit adultery. They progress into a state of mind that leads to the hideous sin. Here are adultery's four phases:

1. Mental infidelity occurs first—Adultery begins in the inner person, the mind, and the emotions.

For out of the heart proceed evil thoughts, murders, adulteries, fornications, thefts, false witness, blasphemies (Matthew 15:19, NKJV).

These wicked designs come from the center of a man's being, from his heart and mind (Mark 7:21; 1 Corinthians 10:4-5). The apostle Peter warns that our eyes are not to be full of adultery because we will not be able to cease from sin (2 Peter 2:14). Jesus said whoever looks on a woman has already committed adultery (Matthew 5:28). The Greek word translated "look" means a continual habit of life. It refers to a man's thinking being continually dominated by an evil fantasy with a particular person. A glance does not equal adultery. Mental infidelity occurs when a man's mind repeatedly previews the desired action in a fantasy. Jesus condemned the practice of centering your attention on a particular person with the intent to commit adultery.

Christians cannot just shift their brains into neutral and hope for good thoughts. They must discipline their minds and fill their minds with righteous thoughts concerning the person they are thinking about (Phil. 4:8).

2. Feeding the flesh magnifies adulterous thoughts— Leaders need to be careful about what they fill their eyes with. Any reading material that excites sexual desire, lust, or fantasy should be eliminated. The Bible exhorts believers to cast off all the works of darkness and not to walk in wantonness (Romans 13:12-13).

Many television shows and videos dramatize and sensationalize immorality, illicit sex, and nudity. Immoral scenes feed fantasies into people's imaginations, which need to be cleansed and disciplined.

Thoughts steer actions. A man's thoughts will shape his character. The mind is like a garden. It can be cultivated to produce the harvest you want. The mind is like a workshop, where important decisions for life and eternity are made. The mind is like an armory, where weapons are forged to win victories. And the mind is like a battlefield, where decisive battles of life are won or lost.

3. Temptations appear—Hidden thoughts will be revealed through a temptation to the flesh. Temptation is not sin, but yielding to the temptation is.

Every man is tempted when he is drawn away by his *own* lust and enticed [by his *own* lusts] (James 1:14).

Abstain from fleshly lusts which war against the soul (1 Peter 2:11, NKJV).

Carefully monitor friendships with the opposite sex. Hugs that last too long excite romantic emotions, and having too many intimate conversations can be dangerous. Avoid flirting with adultery. Your mind and body are your servants. You must discipline them and bring them into order. Keep aloof from fleshly lusts. They campaign against your soul. The body is the servant of the mind.

4. A single act or a planned program?—There is a difference between a person who stumbles in a single adulterous act and one who repeatedly sins following a planned program and shows regret only when he is caught.

King David committed adultery although he was not an adulterer. He stumbled, he repented, he was cleansed, and he had to live with the consequences of his sin. He was overtaken in a trespass.

If a man is overtaken in any trespass, you who are spiritual restore such a one in a spirit of gentleness (Galatians 6:1, NKJV).

If a man stumbles and does something foolish in an act of weakness and falls into sin—even if it is adultery—he can be restored. Certain walls of restraint broke down that need rebuilding. However, an adulterer is habitually involved in immoral acts. He is not stumbling. He uses deceit and strategic, evil planning. It is his lifestyle. An adulterer feeds on the emotions of weak women, understands their makeup, and goes out of his way to seduce them. He looks at members of the opposite sex and fantasizes about acts of adultery with them. He seduces them while counseling, while involved in ministry, or while traveling on business. This person has sold himself and his body to the pleasures of immorality.

CONSEQUENCES OF ADULTERY

Adultery exacts a high price from its participants. It carries great consequences. Esau sold and could not retrieve his birthright because he was a profane man—a fornicator (Hebrews 12:16-17).

Reuben forfeited his birthright because he was a fornicator and had committed incest (Genesis 49:3-4). David committed adultery and murder. He was pardoned but also was punished. The sword never left his house. The Lord raised up evil against his house. David was openly rebuked and humiliated. Amnon committed incest and was assassinated for it. Absalom had lain with his father's wives in his rebellion and died for it. Solomon had many wives who turned his heart away from the Lord. Once that happened, he could not find satisfaction or enjoy life. Numbers, chapter 25, records a period of immorality between the Israelites and Midianites. God brought judgment upon them. Phinehas, who was zealous for the holiness of God, tried to stop it, but God brought the consequences of their immorality upon the whole nation.

Sin may be enjoyable, but it is never successfully covered. No amount of prayer or pious living is going to undo the damage caused by undisciplined actions of infidelity.

He will accept no recompense, nor will he be

appeased though you give many gifts (Proverbs 6:35, NKJV).

An adulterer shall not go unpunished for his sin.

Immediately he went after her, as an ox goes to the slaughter, or as a fool to the correction of the stocks, till an arrow struck his liver. As a bird hastens to the snare, he did not know it would take his life (Proverbs 7:22-23, NKJV).

He is snared like a bird and the end of his snare will be death. The Beck translation of Hebrews 13:4 states, "Those who sin sexually, whether single or married, God will judge."

The adulterer receives the following consequences, according to Proverbs, chapter 6 (NKJV):

- He shall not be innocent. (vs. 29)
- He destroys his own soul. (vs. 32)
- He receives wounds and dishonor. (vs. 33)
- He receives a reproach that will not be wiped away. (vs. 33)

Additional consequences:

- He ruins his friendships.
- He sins against his own body.
- He could possibly be judged with a death penalty.
- He may experience broken fellowship with God's people and excommunication.
- He may give himself to immorality so completely that he becomes reprobate.

Leaders must see hope for change. They must experience genuine conviction, confession, repentance, and cleansing from any sin of immorality or impurity. They must rebuild moral restraints in their lives and break off any immoral relationships. They need to be alert to friendships that could lead to immoral or adulterous relationships.

Quit rationalizing. Quit thinking divorce is the answer to your own marriage problems. Rebuild your marriage carefully. Ask other leaders to stand with you. Become accountable. The best advice is useless against strong temptation unless it is thoroughly taken to heart and translated into habits for right living.

> *Therefore let him who thinks he stands take heed lest he fall.*
> 1 CORINTHIANS 10:12, NKJV

AFTERWORD

*W*e have examined the importance of character development and how a leader must exhibit innate qualities that reflect God's character in every situation and toward all people. Major areas of character development include spiritual, personal, home, social, educational, ministerial, marital, and financial. At times, the development of a person's character may result in great emotional, physical, or financial costs.

We have also evaluated the character development and leadership example of Paul, who exhorted leaders to be above reproach, gentle, of good temperament, respectable, hospitable, teachable, generous, free from the entanglements of money and possessions, reputable, a lover of good, and so on. From Paul, we glean that the success of leadership will not be in the running of the race, but in the finishing. This should be the goal of every leader. The race of character development must be run according to the rules established by God, who has called us to fulfill His great purposes.

Finally, we have examined the area of moral purity in the life of a leader. In an age and culture where immorality is rampant, God's leaders must be careful to guard themselves from secret sins, impure thinking, and defiling habits. Instead, they must be diligent to daily apply the blood of Jesus to their sins, walking before God in true holiness. A life of character is a life of holiness.

As a leader, you must run according to the non-negotiable resolves to which you are committed. Make the decision today to uphold the following 21 resolves that mark a leader:

1. I resolve to govern my life by the principle of purity. *(1 Corinthians 7:1; 1 Peter 1:15-17; 1 Corinthians 9:27; Romans 12:1-2; Philippians 4:8-9; 1 Peter 1:14-15)*

2. I resolve to govern my life by submitting to all levels of godly authority. *(1 Corinthians 10:8; Matthew 7:28)*

3. I resolve to hold my faith in God and His word. *(Joshua 24:15; Hebrews 4:12; 2 Timothy 3:16; Luke 16:17)*

4. I resolve to hold on to the God-thoughts coming to me every day. *(Jeremiah 29:11-12; Psalm 85:8; John 10:27)*

5. I resolve to hold my spirit above the words and ideas of men. *(1 Timothy 1:6; 1 Corinthians 2:4-5; I Thessalonians 2:6-7; Romans 12:1-2)*

6. I resolve to hold my vision to see beyond the immediate into the eternal. *(2 Corinthians 4:17; 1 Corinthians 2:9-10)*

7. I resolve to hold my faith perspective, seeing the best things in the worst times. *(Daniel 3:16-18; Hebrews 11:1-3)*

8. I resolve to hold a relentless pursuit for true biblical revival. *(Hosea 10:12; Psalm 85:6)*

9. I resolve to hold my passion for building an impacting local church. *(Matthew 16:18-20; Acts 2:37-47)*

10. I resolve to hold onto the mantle God is making for me. *(I Kings 19:16-21; II Kings 2:13-15; Jeremiah 17:10; Luke 9:62)*

11. I resolve to hold on to the call of becoming a reformer for my generation. *(Genesis 7:1; Judges 2:10; Esther 4:14)*

12. I resolve to hold my covenant relationships all the days of my life. *(2 Samuel 18:3; 2 Chronicles 23:1)*

13. I resolve to hold an advancing spirit, rejecting any attitudes of retreat. *(Exodus 14:16; Philippians 4:8-11)*

14. I resolve to hold my heart toward the harvest of lost and unchurched people. *(John 4:35; Matthew 9:35-37)*

15. I resolve to hold my "never give up" spirit and attitude. *(Galatians 6:9; Proverbs 24:10; John 19:30; 2 Timothy 4:7; Micah 7:7-8; Proverbs 24:16)*

16. I resolve to hold my *God*-given dream-seeds by faith. *(Proverbs 13:12; Deuteronomy 1:21; Proverbs 4:23; Genesis 37:1-10)*

17. I resolve to destroy all strongholds of my mind which hinder the work of God. *(2 Corinthians 10:3-5; Romans 12:1)*

18. I resolve to endure life contradictions by faith and prayer. *(2 Corinthians 6:1-4; James 4:7-10)*

19. I resolve to steadfastly hold to my commitment to see miracles and the supernatural today. *(Hebrews 13:8; Judges 6:13; 1 Corinthians 12:10,28; Galatians 3:5)*

20. I resolve to hold a forgiving spirit to all, for anything, at all times. *(Matthew 18:21-22; Matthew 18:32-34; Matthew 6:14-15; Hebrews 12:15; Ephesians 4:30-32)*

21. I resolve to hold my integrity as the most important achievement of life and ministry. *(Genesis 20:5-6; I Kings 9:4; Job 27:5; Psalm 25:21; Psalm 26:1; Psalm 78:72; Proverbs 10:9)*

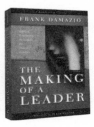

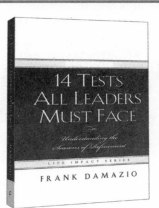

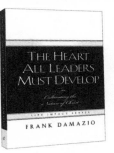
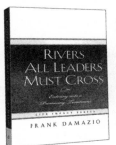

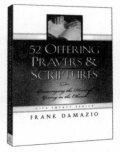

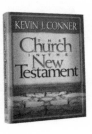

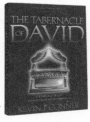